Walking the Ghostly Spaces of Bedford Springs:

The Movement of Presence

John G. Sabol

I.P.E. Research Center

~ John G. Sabol ~

Also by John Sabol...

Ghost Excavator (2007)
Ghost Culture (2007)
Gettysburg Unearthed (2007)
Battlefield Hauntscape (2008)
The Anthracite Coal Region (2008)
The Politics of Presence (2008)
Bodies of Substance, Fragments of Memory (2009)
Phantom Gettysburg (2009)
Digging Deep (2009)
The Re-Haunting(s) of Gettysburg (2010)
The Haunted Theatre (2011)
Ghost Culture Too (2012)
Beyond the Paranormal (2012)
Digging-Up Ghosts (2nd publishing, 2013)
Burnside Bridge (2013)
The Gettysburg Experience (2013)
The Absence Above, A Presence Below (2013)
The Production of Haunted Space (2013)
Centralia, Pennsylvania (2013)
The Ghost Excavation (2013)
The Good Death and the Civil War (2014)
Centralia: A Vision of Ruin (2014)
Altered States: Making the Extraordinary
Ordinary Again (2014)
Archaeology and Ghost Research: A Relational Entanglement (2014)
Performances in Haunted Space: An Afterlife in Ruin (2014)
Haunting Presences, Ruins, and Ghostly Entanglements (2015)
The Afterlife of Centralia: Presences in a Landscape of
Destruction (2015)
An Archaeology Without Borders: Performance Excavations in
Embedded/Entangled Fields (2016)
Ghost Hunt: Exploding the Myths/Exploring the Possibility (2016)
The Haunting of the Omni Bedford Springs Resort and Spa (2016)
The Haunting Presences of the Omni Bedford Springs (2017)
Victorian Ghosts of the Omni Bedford Springs:
Representation and Reveal (2017)

Walking the Ghostly Spaces of Bedford Springs:

The Movement of Presence

Ghost Excavator Books, Inc. ™©

Bedford, Pennsylvania,
USA

~ *John G. Sabol* ~

ISBN-13: 978-1974093663
ISBN-10: 1974093662

Ghost Excavation Books, Inc.™©
A division of C.A.S.P.E.R. Research Center™©,
Bedford, PA, USA

<u>Photo 1: Is This the Image of a Haunted Location?</u>

Preface

In this book an emphasis is placed on an archaeological approach to a haunted building complex. Within its walls, multiple layers of construction, functionality, social occupation, cultural tradition, memory, and presence are present (and materializing). The Omni Bedford Springs and Spa complex is viewed as a tangible and material 'bricolage', or haunted 'brick (and limestone) collage' of past presences. Its historical evolution of (and 'revolutionary') sociability has created and enabled different senses of place (as experience and memory) to become embedded and attached to a constructed social reality of this well-known tourist destination.

Through a mapping of its perceived haunted spaces (see Sabol 2016), linked to a review of historical material culture and human presence, the building's haunted rooms and corridors take center stage. A theatrics of sensual materializations attests to the interrelationship of the various socio-cultural contexts in which the building and grounds, and its rooms, hallways, and historical displays are inserted.

The main building, the original 'Stone Inn' (constructed 1810), and its annexes running horizontally in both directions, and vertically upward through various floors of construction, accumulate (and sometimes hide) these layers of memory, until materializing in the form of a 'ghostly presence'. At the core of the complex is a biographical narrative of place that permits the contemporary guest access to the multiplicity of stories, situations, events, and individual and group narratives that have become imprinted onto the spaces of the hotel and spa complex. These come in various forms, such as the historical displays of documents and photographs, the antique furniture, the historical tours, and the recent addition of 'ghost tours' there (see Sabol 2017a).

<u>Photo 2: Bedford Springs Historical Display</u>

Not all haunted locations need be in ruin and unoccupied. Even a fully-functioning and popular destination, such as the Bedford Springs Hotel and Spa complex, has 'room' for former, returning guests as 'ghostly presences'. The ghost stories of Bedford Springs, like all biographies, have their gaps in occupancy. This is the normal process of remembering and forgetting, relevant in the understanding of memory, and the politics involved in the quiet (and sometimes reluctant) acknowledgement of the site's haunted heritage.

The site's biographical metaphor is an archaeological tool. It allows us to incorporate objects and things as active agents in the construction of the social (Gosden and Marshall 1999). It is this social aspect that allows contemporary guests to sometimes become 'witnesses' to the ghostly presences of Bedford Springs. There are many objects (historical documents, décor, furniture, historical photographs and postcards, even 'inscribed' window panes) that continue to resonate with the presences of the past. In a previous book (Sabol 2017b), I examined the association between this material culture and the presence of Late Victorian and Early Edwardian 'ghosts' at Bedford Springs.

The biography of a place, and the biography of historical material culture in place at Bedford Springs, intersects with the 'afterlife' biography of its ghosts. All of this presence, and memory of presence there, is interwoven together into a sensory bundle in which the hauntings and ghostly presences are embedded in the Bedford Springs' historical present.

Similar to an archaeological excavation, the ghost tours 'unearth', through storytelling, the manifesting presence of the past in contemporary settings. The ghost tour emphasizes a 'haunting' historicity, through these tales of materializing 'vestiges' (or 'artifacts") of presence. During the tours, participating guests have reported sensing these presences, even photographing them (for examples, see Sabol 2017a).

Such 'in situ' emergences produce their own (additional) ghost stories. Thus, the haunting is part of a process of contemporary interest, exposure, and contact of presence becoming present. Though physical and social changes re-occur frequently at Bedford Springs, this palimpsest of cumulative haunting phenomena remains embedded in its own biographical strata, principally the Late Victorian and Early Edwardian eras.

Bedford Springs is a 'ruin', in fragmented form, of multiple pasts that continue to 'haunt' the present. This ruined, largely unobserved, layers of 'haunting' strata is part of the contemporary archaeological record of Bedford Springs. Guests can access it through the interactive nature of our ghost tours. We not only tell the story, we add historical and social context, and we provide the guests with means to encounter these ghosts (see Sabol 2017b). This affords the guests the opportunity to experience first-hand these ephemeral, but recurring, haunting phenomena. It also permits the guest to become a co-producer of knowledge about 'what' (and 'who') continues to 'haunt' the Bedford Springs environment.

The contemporary guest, as ghost tour participant, can document this archaeological 'footprint' of a haunting becoming present. These ghost stories allow us to re-construct Bedford Springs where 'history' still exists in spaces, and where, in some sense, past activities are still occurring. The Bedford Springs is a place where contemporary and past guests wander into one another. By identifying fragments of stories about the past, one on top of another in the same space, ghostly tales allow us to re-configure conditions for the possibility of presence in the present.

Table of Contents

Photographs

Introduction: Walking the Ghostly Spaces of Bedford Springs

Photo 3: The Ghost Tour

Walking around is fundamental to the everyday practice (and experience) of social life, especially the social life of a popular tourist destination such as Bedford Springs. But can contemporary social life be extended to walking back <u>toward</u> (and with) the 'ghosts' of prior occupants of the same social touristic space?

A walk is an experience of a performance in space. Sometimes, that performance becomes an echo from the past, a hiccup of time that enfolds contemporary reality. Such a walk is a mapping, not a travel description. It locates presence. During an 'investigative' walk, one may encounter a 'crypto-sapien', a still unexplained type of human form, a 'ghost'. Whether that space of encounter then becomes perceived as 'haunted' is irrelevant. What is relevant, and what becomes unique, are the mixtures of influences that combine to form particular spaces, uncannily understood. A 'ghost tour' (as an interpretative walk) assimilates more completely these mixtures.

This type of walk is not about spatial distance. It is about time, and the layers of memory along the way. It is about the past, present, and future, and the liminal 'times' in between. It is a period of 'stoppages' and 'presences', a sensory itinerary that begins in the past, one that presently continues, and one that manifests in the future:

"To follow a route is to accept an interpretation…to walk the same way is to reiterate something deep; to move through the same space the same way is a means of becoming the same person, thinking the same thoughts. It's a form of spatial theater…".

- Rebecca Solnit, *A History of Walking.*

Walking Bedford Springs is more than just about movement. It is about walking in spaces that continue to move memories, ones that embed time as guests pass thru time. Walking the Bedford Springs building complex is walking in rhythm to past stories, those that remain attached there as the "ghosts of place". These presences are predecessors, former guests who leave 'footprints' that others, as contemporary visitors, can still follow. These 'footprints', as a forensic sensorium, are notices of presence, an acknowledgement that some memories accumulate and continue to 'haunt' a place.

Bedford Springs is not a mathematically-calculated set of spaces to be probed and measured by 'ghost hunters'. Changes in temperature, humidity, electromagnetic fields (EMF), etc., do not tell stories. These measurements are not relative to why presences, in the form of past guests, still remain attached to the place. A ghost hunting, tech-focused, approach cannot humanize the place or the haunting. Instead, it leaves the 'guests', as former socio-cultural beings, out of a haunting. It raises, not the dead, but the level of presence to a 'paranormal' event. Such a proposed event cannot explain the movements of perceived haunting phenomena.

Places such as Bedford Springs are contexts for human experiences. These experiences are constructed in movement, memory, encounter, and association. Bedford Springs is a place in which social spaces move people emotionally. It was (is) a location where "best friends forever" met, interacted, and are remembered. It is a place that 'attracted' people, still attracts them. This social relationality cannot be measured by ghost hunting electronic devices.

Sociability and its remembrance has nothing to do with 'movements' on a meter.

In its simplest form, this involves stories (albeit 'ghost stories'), and a storyteller (the 'ghost'). A haunting manifestation is given meaning through a materialization that requires the performance of a particular action. DeCerteau (1984) states that every story not only involves some kind of temporal movement, but also a spatial practice. This spatial practice, I propose, is cultural in character.

A ghost's story also requires a sense of sensual presence, relative to time, one having cultural meaning. It is socially, context-specific, and is not related to a 'ghost-hunting' environmental deviation. The ghost stories at Bedford Springs are all about the movements and social practices of past guests there. When stories are linked to regularly (and repeated) spatial practices, the practices, together with the stories, become embedded into a place as a relational entanglement. The stories, as ghost stories, and the place, as Bedford Springs, help to construct and reproduce each other through time.

Places, like people, have biographies. They are constructed, utilized, and remembered in relation to continuing practices. In many ways, Bedford Springs reiterates many past practices enacted there. This connects the ghost stories, a biography formed in the past, to what is manifesting today and what can be sensed by contemporary guests and staff.

These ghost stories are organized as a 'ghost tour' in which guests move through various spaces of the hotel complex. Haunted spaces acquire material reference points that can be visited and experienced. They become spaces in which the social, ones once thought dead and past, are reproduced and can be explored in the present. These ghost stories represent a non-conventional, but still historical and ethnographic, means of organizing the meaning of what Bedford Springs represents both in the past and today.

The 'ghosts' at Bedford Springs leave sensual 'traces', brief 'stories' that tell tales that include sounds, smells, sight, and touch. These traces are experienced at Bedford Springs as one casually moves through the hotel complex, when one is being entertained, or is entertaining. These are movements between past and present, walking into uncertain time and out of a certain one. The hauntings do not re-enact stories that are already history, but rather keeps those stories (and memories) moving forward, always present, into the future. In doing so, the hauntings and their associated ghostly presences portray a vivid, uncanny belonging and attachment to the Bedford Springs.

This suggests that to 'walk the Springs' is far more distant (yet close) than what is registered on the ground as those sounds of footsteps moving from one present location to another. It suggests that a walk there becomes the exclusive property to properly experience a haunting ephemeral moment there. A pure walking mode, however, can convey little or nothing of embodied experience. To make sense of the haunting spaces there, one must take the time to sense the change of time and presence, as one moves from the present into the past, and back again.

There should be no predisposition to anticipate something happening. This allows for a context in which to place an encounter, one unanticipated, or, in the case of the ghost tour, to resonate (for a time) with prior guests. This book is a self-guided tour, or a format that can be used as one participates in the weekly Bedford Springs 'ghost tour' that is offered every Saturday night at 10:00 p.m. However, both formats (self or guided) require some kind of location attunement, such that movement, history, experience, and manifestation are grounded in a shared relational bundle, one that is related to particular spaces at Bedford Springs.

One cannot simply walk into another world (contrary to pop culture portrayals). One walks with, not into, the past. This personal immersion does not imply a face-to-face encounter with a ghost. It means heading the same way, sharing the same vistas and activities as those of the past, and retreating from outside, distractive influences that are contemporary (not past). Bedford Springs is certainly a place to dis-attach oneself. It is also a location that continues to resonate with what occurred in the past there. Today's guests enjoy many of the same activities that were often experienced and entertained by past guests.

A relationship between walking, embodied experience, and sociability is crucial. One relationship is the routine of 'getting around' and another is the uncanny feeling of someone being there. This duality allows us to comprehend a place as both the creation of flows and routes of movement between past and present. A place walked through is made (and re-made) by the interaction of people and space. Those who frequent Bedford Springs (returning again and again) create 'habit memories' of movements, behaviors, and experiences. This involves a rhythm of place, some of which may remain as imprints on the environment.

A particular 'sensescape' is created. Such an environment brings a closeness, a bond between people who stay (have stayed) at Bedford Springs, allowing a physical and sensual co-presence to develop and evolve there. Layers of experience and memory are created, characterized by a commonality in movements and social acts.

This sensual layering is significant because it means that as rooms and functions are added (along with décor and technological change), it creates a stratigraphy of experience and memory, some of which becomes embedded onto the place. This suggests potentially multiple layers of haunting and ghostly presences, all embedded and attached to the surface of the contemporary setting. That is why a guide is both useful and needed, and why this book was written.

Movement implies observation. To understand a haunted location, however, implies a different understanding of movement and observation. A haunting is not something in place where everything is laid out, an 'in situ' experience. A 'real' haunting, one that is interactive not simply a 'recording' (residual), is the manifestation of a sense of presence. This involves the process of <u>becoming</u> <u>present</u>. This is production, not transportation. It is not something that exists in place, as a 'display' of ghostly presence, such as those historical displays that are placed in the 'Duke of Bedford Library' and in other rooms.

One does not move, and enter a certain location and space, observing the 'haunting' displayed there. Observation centers on the kind of involvement that is required for there to become present a past presence in the contemporary environment. This is the 'classic' anthropological fieldwork concept of participant-observation. It means being attentive to how one acts in particular spaces, observing while moving through a space without being constrained by what is there in a particular space today.

In the movements through the Bedford Springs landscape, there is something gained by a sensible and sensitive walk-through. A relational world of impressions, signs of presence, and physicality can be experienced, ones that do not conform to contemporary expectations. This must be felt, not measured by some 'ghost hunting' electronic device or phone app. In this process of participating movements, Bedford Springs unfolds its <u>continuing</u> history, and unravels its ghosts. Observation becomes a movement through lives lived there, and experiences that are still remembered of the place.

If Bedford Springs is experienced through a set of participation/observation movements, it follows that an understanding of the place and its ghostly presences must become meaningful through an acknowledgement of, and knowledge of, previous experiences in present contexts: a 'haunting' space and text (as a 'ghost story") that is attached, and situated on the surface of the contemporary environment. There is no 'room' to measure environmental deviations in this relational context. What 'deviates' is not humidity or temperature, but rather cultural expression.

So let us begin the tour….

The tour beings in the most recent spaces of Bedford Springs, the Spa area, and proceeds from there through the spatial layers of history and haunting. We will end the tour in the oldest occupied section of the resort, the original hotel area once known as the "Stone Inn" (1810). What this movement through space and time demonstrates is that the hauntings do not necessarily conform to the age of the building construction. It is not the physical structure that haunts today's guests. It is the spaces in which functions have changed through time.

The original construction moved out of the original "Stone Inn" both horizontally (in both directions), and vertically upward. The distribution of haunting presences are not accumulative: more in the older continuously-occupied spaces; less in the newer spaces. It is proposed that the hauntings are based on past activities that were performed in particular spaces, themselves dependent upon the 'uniqueness' of the activity that was entertained there, not the amount of activities that were enacted there. The 'uniqueness' of these particular spaces and activities will be mentioned throughout this guided 'ghost tour'. Finally, none of these hauntings are associated with any tragic event (that took lives) that occurred at Bedford Springs.

The Tour:
The Ground Floor -
The Spa Area

More than any 'other', it is the presence of Late Victorian and Early Edwardian (1890-1910) women that haunt Bedford Springs. This is no mere uncanny coincidence. These ghosts haunt Bedford Springs for a reason, and it is not negative or evil.

In the examination of Victorian ghost stories, Vanessa D. Dickerson (1996) provides a possible reason for the predominance of Victorian female ghosts at Bedford Springs. Women in middle class Victorian homes were often invisible, taken for granted, "barely there", and pushed into the background (1996:11).

Not so at Bedford Springs, where women had 'unique' experiences. Bedford Springs was a place where they were fully visible, alongside men in various activities.

Photo 4: Victorian Women at Bedford Springs

<u>Photo 5: Victorian Women at Bedford Springs</u>

These Bedford Springs Victorian women certainly were never 'barely there'! At Bedford Springs, Victorian female presence belongs there. Bedford Springs today has become what Late Victorian psychical researchers termed "phantasmogenetic centres". The female Victorian ghost defines the existence of a haunted Bedford Springs.

The feelings of presence, and the materializations of absent presences (the female Victorian ghost) becomes a means of communication between the Victorian past at Bedford Springs and the present, between the Victorians and contemporary guests. It becomes a means of looking with the ghost, and looking at this Late Victorian/Early Edwardian world at Bedford Springs. It is a form of 'excavating' Victorian presence.

Photo 6: The Tour begins here…

We begin the tour with the perceived presence of a Victorian-era female who is seen sitting in a chair in a small lounge area near elevator 6 and stairs in the spa section.

Photo 7: The Spa Lounge area

Is she gazing at the wall opposite where she is seen seated, where 'picture postcards' from that period are displayed? Why else would she be sitting there? In her time, this was open space, located between the building which housed the kitchen and the indoor pool/solarium.

Photo 8: The Original Location of the Haunting

If she is sitting there, gazing at these 'picture postcards', she is no residual presence. She is 'interacting' with the contemporary, <u>not</u> the past physical environment. Be careful, do not frighten her. Usually, as someone approaches to take the elevator (late at night), she vanishes.

After this 'storied' space, the tour moves down the corridor, now the location of the "Bedford Market", the "Tally-Ho", the "Exercise Room" and "Harriet Lane's", toward older sections of the resort.

Photo 9: The Hallway

The tour stops near the pool restrooms. Here, on the wall, is a display of photographs which depict the original 1905 indoor pool. It is here that we begin to tell the tour participants the stories of those presences that 'haunt' the indoor pool, including a little girl from the Early Edwardian era named "Anna" or "Hanna".

Here, we also talk about the haunted "Ladies Bathroom". Why is it that the Ladies (not the Men's) restroom is haunted? This is not the only Ladies Restroom that appears haunted at Bedford Springs (see below). Why is it that only certain women 'feel' the touch (on their legs) of a 'ghostly' presence there? Is it because they are wearing pants (not a dress), not a 'typical' or 'fashionable' woman's clothing of that era?

Is this 'ghostly' touch, a phantom fashion statement, part of Edwardian social etiquette, or simply a child's curiosity? Whichever you choose to believe, be alert to this presence, if you are wearing pants as you enter there, especially late at night.

We next enter the contemporary entrance to the indoor pool, walking through the door, and proceed into the solarium. Here, various ghost stories are told of the 'haunting' of the indoor pool space.

<u>Photo 10: The Solarium</u>

Guests, while on the tour, have taken photos here in which various images of people have appeared. The most frequent image photographed is that of a male, who has a moustache and is wearing a hat. He has been photographed in various spaces in and around the glass doors, located on the opposite end to the solarium. This location was the original pool entrance back in the early 20th century.

<u>Note:</u> When taking photos, entities do not always appear at once. Sometimes, a day or even weeks pass before a presence is seen. Please periodically review your photos.

In the solarium, we talk to the participants about the best locations to take photographs. At the end of the tour, we show the guests a photo, taken in February 2017, of two 'full-bodied' ghostly presences in the pool area. One of these, the man with the hat and moustache, has been photographed by various guests while on the ghost tour.

The 2nd floor balcony, facing the pool and solarium, once the site where small musical ensembles played while guests swam in the pool, is especially 'hauntingly' active. A female, dressed in the style of the late 1940's (or early 1950's) has been seen there. It is said she appears to be listening to music. A woman, in Victorian dress, has been photographed ascending the stairs there. The 2nd Floor Balcony, a dark shadow figure has been seen and photographed by an associate in Housekeeping.

Photo 11: The 2nd Floor Balcony

Exiting the indoor pool, the tour moves down the corridor, once an outdoor space, past the "Que Sera Sera" snack area. We are now in the corridor between "Que Sera Sera" and the "Duke of Bedford Library".

Photo 12: The Corridor

In the mid-1950's, this space was called "Reynold's Bar", named after James Reynolds who painted the murals (now gone) in the adjacent bar lounge area, now the "Duke of Bedford Library". James Reynolds was also an author. He penned a number of books on tourism, and also three books on ghosts. In one, *Ghosts in American Houses,* was published in 1955, the same year the murals were painted. In this book, he says the following:

"Persons frequently ask me, 'Mr. Reynolds, have *you* ever seen a ghost'? The answer is: 'Hundreds of ghosts, all over the world'. More than a century ago, four men were strung from the crossbeam of an old barn at Waterford, Vermont. They are still there. Believe me or not – it is as you choose – I saw their figures silhouetted in the moonlight *before* ever I heard the story…" (1955: Introduction).

Photo 13: Reynolds Bar

Like most spaces at Bedford Springs, the area of the former "Reynolds Bar" and lounge served various functions in the long history of Bedford Springs. Today's "Duke of Bedford Library", for example, besides being the lounge for "Reynolds Bar", was also a music room and a place where billiards was played. On its window panes (not original to the room), a number of etchings can be found. They include names and dates of former guests. These were originally located in other areas of the resort complex, but were placed in the "Library" to complement the historical displays.

Most of the etchings date to the Late Victorian and Early Edwardian Periods. As a remembrance of former 'engagements' enacted at the hotel, do they today serve as 'memory cues' for past presences who remain attached to the 'engagement ceremony'? At this location, we have recorded a number of audio manifestations ('EVP'), occurring during scenarios we enacted as 'simming' marriage proposals.

In the "Reynolds Bar" area, we have also recordings of activity there, including one male voice that clearly said, "can I have another".

Was he referring to 'another' book (as the "Duke of Bedford Library"), or 'another' drink, when it was Reynolds Bar"? Also in this area a guest 'witnessed' a visual anomaly, as she was listening to our ghost stories.

She was looking at the glass door and the indoor pool, at the original entrance, when she saw pass two females dressed in what appears to be Bedford Springs staff attire (though not contemporary clothing). They were walking, with arms spread out, carrying sets of white towels. Both were full-bodied 'apparitions'. Each had their hair in a bun, reminiscent of the Early Edwardian Period. Was this a residual manifestation of former Bedford Springs' staff?

Proceeding past the "Duke of Bedford Library", on the left is the entrance to the "Crystal Dining Room". Here are displayed photographs of former guests. These photos of young men and women were taken during the Late Victorian/Early Edwardian Period (1880-1910). Guests in the photos are dressed differently, as they appear in various 'staged' poses (and activities). The photos are enlarged, coming from other photos that are distributed throughout the hotel complex.

This suggests that the photos were taken at different times. Did these particular guests frequent ('haunt') Bedford Springs during the Victorian Era? Do some of them remain, attached to their 'Bedford Springs Experience'?

Photo 14: The "Crystal Dining Room"

Two individuals whose photos are displayed here may be the same individuals who now 'haunt' the indoor pool. This is based on the physical likeness between the pool photo (taken in February 2017) and the photos taken in the 1890's of these two guests. Guests on the tour have also commented on their similarity.

Some guests on the tour, those who have dined in the Crystal Dining Room, have stated to us that the Victorian photo displays there have affected them while eating. They (the photos) appear to have an 'animated' appearance. Some tour guests have identified one particular photo as especially 'haunting'. This is the photo of the man, in various poses and attire, who we think is one of the men who appears in the 2017 pool photo.

In the "Crystal Dining Room", after dining hours while staff are preparing for the next day's dining experience, some have reported hearing hushed conversations and the 'clinking' of glasses and silverware on plates. When the staff member stops to listen, the 'noise' also stops. It begins again when staff continue with their work activities.

In the "Daniel Webster Room" there, a number of anomalies have been reported by both staff and tour participants. These include the smell of cigars that permeates most of the room at times (note: Bedford Springs is a smoke-free facility). Conversations are also heard, and there are two reports of the appearance of 'Daniel Webster' himself (based on his portrayed image hanging on the wall in a picture frame in the room). This was reported by one member of staff who works in the "Crystal Dining Room", and one female 'sensitive' who participated in one of our tours.

Some female tour participants have felt 'uneasy' in this room, and more than one has left the room because of the uncanny atmosphere felt there. Females are asked not to ask 'Mr. Webster' a question, or to ask him for a cigar or shot of whiskey, as some female tour participants have done. It appears that the 'presence' in the room does not like to 'entertain' females.

Photo 15: The "Daniel Webster Room"

The next location on the tour is the "Grand Staircase" in the main lobby area. There are several reports of staff hearing footsteps on these stairs when no one is observed there. The sounds of someone walking on these stairs has also been reported by security when Bedford Springs was closed in the 1990's due to major flooding there.

Photo 16: The "Grand Staircase"

The First Floor

At the top of the "Grand Staircase" is the "Colonnade Ballroom" which at one time was the original "Crystal Dining Room". When functioning in that capacity, it was the largest dining room east of the Mississippi River. During World War II, it served as the administrative headquarters for the Keystone Training School which instructed sailors on the operation and use of various electronic equipment. More than 7,000 sailors graduated from the school between the years 1942-44.

<u>Photo 17: The "Colonnade Ballroom"</u>

To the left of the ballroom entrance, as you ascend the stairs, is a hat display. One of these hats (shown in the photo below) has been seen by three different people (on three separate occasions) on a women dressed in Victorian clothing. She has been observed walking down the hallway in front of the "Colonnade Ballroom", proceeding through the doorway, turning right into the present "First Ladies Lounge". There, she stops and disappears.

Photo 18: The hat worn by the Lady in Victorian dress

Braude (1991) proposes that "an apparition is a real, localized externalized entity, and not simply a subjective construct of the percipient' (1991:194). The 'Victorian' lady wearing the hat fits this description since she has been seen repeatedly and independently by different people over time in the same location (Braude 1991). None of the witnesses to this 'apparition', however have checked to see if the hat in the display, worn by this 'apparition', was missing.

The "First Ladies Lounge", previously the "Garden Room", is also haunted. Audio recordings of subdued conversations have been heard. The sounds of glasses and cutlery being moved about (with no one present) have also been heard. We have also recorded a male voice there saying the following: "Ike here". We assumed he was referring to President Eisenhower, so we stated that he must be surrounded by security. A male voice (the same one previously recorded) answered "Marines".

When it was the "Garden Room", the wall facing the hillside and the "Cottage" (now the Administrative Offices) did not exist. This area was an open balcony, at the end of which was a fountain (with a Lion's Head), serving the "Sweetwater Springs". This fountain can still be seen there.

Photo 19: The "First Ladies Lounge"

The "Administrative Offices" are also haunted. On the 1st floor, the sounds of a person typing are sometimes heard. There is no typewriter in the office.

Photo 20: The "Administration Offices"

To the left of the "Administration Offices" is the present Housekeeping, Laundry, and Engineering sections of Bedford Springs. The upper floor (now gone) once served as the "Presidential Suite". Also, during World War II, the building served as the location where 187 Japanese diplomats from embassies in Europe were briefly housed (August-November 1945). During the interment at Bedford Springs, one elderly Japanese man died of a heart attack. Is he the Japanese man that has been seen walking the corridor toward the restaurant area on the ground floor? Is it just a coincidence that the Japanese man who died of a heart attack was a cook? Is that why he is walking toward the restaurants?

Outside the "First Ladies Lounge" is elevator number 3. It is said to be haunted by a woman in Victorian dress. It is not known why she 'haunts' this particular space, nor what existed in that space before the elevator came into use.

The Second Floor

We climb the stairs to our next stop, the "Eisenhower Ballroom". Here, during World War II, the location was the site of USO dances for the sailors who were in training at the Keystone Training School at Bedford Springs between the years 1942-44.

Photo 21: The "Eisenhower Ballroom"

In the lobby, on the walls, are a series of photographs of the men in training, including one photo of a USO dance there. It has been reported by staff that late at night the sounds of music are heard in the ballroom. The music that is heard is sounds of the Big Band Era, context-specific to WWII. Are these merely residual manifestations, or do interactive 'ghostly presences' still remain attached to the ballroom?

Leaving the main ballroom, and walking toward the main staircase, is an exit door on the left. Once outside, a short walk down the walkway, one can observe to the right (one floor down) one of the Springs' fountains ("Sweetwater"), now tapped off. This was the fountain that was used by guests as they exited the "Garden Room" (the present "First Ladies Lounge") to "take the water".

Photo 22: The "Sweetwater" Spring

Directly in front of you, at the top of the hill, is the "Cottage", the present administrative building of Bedford Springs. In the basement is a small museum, and large walk-in safe. In the building, on the ground floor, staff have heard someone typing on a typewriter. There is no typewriter in the building. Is this just another 'residual' sound, or is there an 'interactive' (perhaps a former staff member) still attached to the building?

<u>Photo 23: The "Cottage"</u>

The Ground Floor-II

The tour continues on the ground floor. We walk past the lobby and reception areas into the tavern hallway, leading toward the restaurant areas ("1796 Restaurant"; "Frontier Tavern"). This space may be the most haunted section of the hotel complex. This is due to the multiple functions and activities, and thus experiences (some unique) and memories, that were 'entertained' in this area.

Photo 24: The 'Haunted' Hallway

In Victorian times, this hallway was an open space, with no walls separating outdoor from indoor. Beneath the roof were a large number of tables where Victorian guests could play various card and table games.

Photo 25: Card-Playing at Bedford Springs

Men and women were of equal status at these tables. This 'liberating' aspect of the "Bedford Springs Experience' may be one of several 'liberating' factors (producing 'embedded' memories) of why many Victorian Era females 'haunt' Bedford Springs (see Sabol 2017 for more examples).

This open hallway was also the scene of summer Victorian lemonade parties, an activity that continued well into the 20th century.

Photo 26: A Victorian "Lemonade Party"

In this space, the 'Germans' or Cotillions' were also held, a social gathering where young men and women would gather, usually in a 'themed' dance.   Is this the location (one of several) where "best friends forever" first met?

Photo 27: A 'Themed' German

Photo 28: Another 'Themed' Dance at Bedford Springs

Did these dances lead, in some instances, to the 'engagement ring etchings' now displayed on window panes in the "Duke of Bedford Library?

Along this hallway, we have recorded the sounds of Morse Code. At the time of the recording, we did not know that the equipment used to train the sailors during WWII was located just down the hallway, in the present "Reagan Ballroom". Was the recording a 'residual' of those training days? Was the 'message', which stated that a ship had been sunk off the Atlantic coast, merely a training exercise or an historical fact? More research is needed to ascertain what the 'message' was about.

Also, in this area, two 'ghostly presences' have been reported. One is an adult female. She is seen walking down the hallway to the present restaurant area. The other is an elderly Japanese man who is also seen walking toward the restaurants.

Was he one of those interred at Bedford Springs (from Japanese embassies in Europe) at the end of WWII? Was he the man who died, of a fatal heart attack in November 1945, during the three month interment? Why is he walking toward the restaurants and the kitchen area? The man who died served as a cook at a Japanese embassy. Is this the reason why he is walking toward the restaurant/kitchen area, or is this mere coincidence? Is his presence merely a 'residual of the past, or is he an interactive 'ghostly presence? These are questions that still need to be investigated and answered.

Our next stop is the "Defibaugh's Table" area, the site of the original "Stone Inn" kitchen. In this eating space, the tables are from the

"Defibaugh's Tavern", which later became the "Willows". The tavern is located three miles east of Bedford Springs. Do these tables contain any 'residual' energies of former patrons? Some people have reported 'shadow' presences in this room.

Photo 29: "Defibaugh's Table"

Are there 'smells' still embedded onto them of the famous "chicken a la Maryland", a broiled chicken dinner using a proprietary recipe? Unfortunately, the recipe for the famous chicken dinner has been lost to time. It was a favorite of Bedford Springs' guests.

Those who stayed at the hotel would travel to the tavern by "Tally-Ho' carriages. It was an occasion for young people to meet and socially interact. Perhaps, some future married couples first met on a "Tally-Ho" excursion? There is a photo of a "Tally-Ho" located on the wall in this room. Do any of these guests remain 'attached' to Bedford Springs and the "Tally-Ho"?

Photo 30: A "Tally-Ho" party

After leaving here, we turn left walking down the narrow hallway toward the restaurant restroom facilities. Once again, as in similar facilities near the indoor pool, it is the Ladies Restroom that is perceived to be haunted. There are various reports that those who enter

"Stall 2" have experienced uncanny phenomena.

It has been reported that someone tries to open the "Stall 2" door, yet, upon inspection, there is no one there. There are also reports of a little girl, in Victorian dress, who is seen throughout the restaurant area, usually late at night. This little girl has been reported to go into the Ladies Restroom, and then disappears from sight.

Is this "Anna" who also is said to 'haunt' the indoor pool? Is she the one who is trying to open "Stall 2" in the Ladies Restroom"? Why? Is she just playing, or does she remember something different that occurred there, before it was a bathroom facility, that arouses her interest?

The final stop on the ghost tour is the space where billiards is now played, located at the far end of the restaurant area.

Photo 31: The "Billiards" Space

There is a photo on the wall there, taken in 1895. It shows the members of the Pennsylvania Bar Association, a group that still comes to (thus 'haunts') Bedford Springs. In the photo, the figure of a young boy can be seen. This boy has been seen, wearing the same clothes, throughout the hotel today. He has also appeared is some recent guests' photographs.

<u>Photo 32: The "Photograph"</u>

So, ends the tour, as of July 2017. The continuation of the ghost tour past July 2017 surely will afford increased haunting phenomena at Bedford Springs. Only time will tell. The Bedford Springs remains 'timeless' in that respect, a place where some former guests remain 'attached'……

Addendum:

Haunting Ambiance and the Phenomenon of 'Affordances': The "Bedford Springs Experience"

What remains at Bedford Springs, in terms of historical guest behavior and resort activity, and what is 'exhibited' there today (as historical artifacts, documents, and décor) are forms of "affordances" (Gibson 2015) for potential haunting phenomena. An affordance is a series of gradations of interrelated processes (and 'cues'), consisting of spaces, objects, and acts of behavior. These request, allow, encourage actions, while others can discourage it.

The importance of an affordance is its ability, in terms of a haunting, to encourage a materialization, or refuse to become present. A full-bodied apparition is one result of a highly-encouraging affordance; while an EVP of "get out" results from a discouraging affordance. An affordance allows memories to be remembered.

Present guest behaviors and historical displays and décor 'afford' ghostly activity in the form of a particular pathway from past to present at Bedford Springs. The Bedford Springs resort retains a resonating relationality between what occurred there in the past, what remains there today, and how the "Bedford Springs Experience" is still an affordance to its past history and guest's memories of the place.

Photo 33: A Resonating 'Affordance'

Photo 34: Another Example of a Resonating 'Affordance'

Despite technological and architectural change, and alterations in specific spatial functionalities, the contemporary guest can <u>still</u> see/do (what was seen and done in the past). This becomes the Bedford Springs affordance.

Talking about past guest activity, and contemporary ghostly manifestations on the ghost tour, also 'encourages continued materializations, and is thus also an 'affordance'. It allows attached presences a way to act, and become part of the contemporary setting. Guests taking photographs, especially on the ghost tour, also encourages ghostly presences to materialize because it is a form of remembrance of how they were photographed in the past.

The use of photography at Bedford Springs is a form of 'targeting' a specific time in the history of the resort. The personal photograph replaced the landscape photograph in the 1880's (at a time when many of the 'personalized' Bedford Springs' photographs were taken) as a symbolic and physical remembrance of one's stay at a location. Thus, photography is an 'encouraging' affordance.

The meaning of the 'hauntings' at Bedford Springs is an enduring relationship of what the "Bedford Springs Experience" <u>still 'affords'</u> its guests, both in the past and the 'hauntingly' present. These hauntings are not what is popularly represented on TV and social media: they are not 'anomalies' or 'paranormal' phenomena. At Bedford Springs, they are logical responses to the Bedford Springs' affordances that remain embedded there.

It is something remembered, a socially-encouraged relationship between former guests and their relation with Bedford Springs. This is the memory of experiences that afforded them to come back again and again, some even after their death. The 'afterlife' is alive and well at Bedford Springs.

The physical and social environment of Bedford Springs, historically-defined as a place of recreation and relaxation, where "best friends forever" met, was (and continues to be) uniquely suited to certain past guests. Some of these became the guests that 'remain' (or have come back). These are the Bedford Springs 'ghosts'. The concept of affordance is an attempt to define what conditions at the

Bedford Springs allowed (or 'afforded') possible 'ghostly presence.

Photo 35: The Social Environment that 'Afforded' Ghostly Presence

What 'holds' (encourages) these 'ghosts' to be here are the 'affordances' of past acts, situations, conversations, displays, and décor of the past in the contemporary setting. The historical displays, exhibited throughout the hotel complex, however, are not merely what is called "canonical affordances" (Costall and

Richards 2013:87): the thing they represent, illustrating the social history of Bedford Springs.

They also serve as 'cues' of remembrance for embedded presences that may still 'haunt' there. Affordances provide meaning, and come into being (as a 'haunting') within the flow of activity that occurs at Bedford Springs, including the re-telling of stories on the ghost tour.

Thus, the tour becomes more than a series of narratives, something to occupy the guest at night or to provide a little 'scary' entertainment. The ghost tour becomes, more importantly, a 'stage' for enacted performances that afford a call to manifest and participate once again in the "Bedford Springs Experience".

The tours afford (or make) present (and future) hauntings possible, not merely locates where a haunting may have occurred (or been perceived) in the past. So, whether you attend the tour or read this book, you become part of a proper role-playing affordance, and the relationality that preserves, develops, and allows to grow these 'haunting' memories of Bedford Springs.

While the environmental setting, and historical displays and décor, encourage certain time periods at the hotel (especially the Victorian Period), they also, at the same time, discourage other times and memories. That is why at Bedford Springs many of the 'ghostly presences' are Late Victorian or Early Edwardian. Bedford Springs, whether intentionally or not, through its displays and décor encourages the presence of these historical periods.

For example, the extensive use of Late Victorian and Early Edwardian personal photographs is a highly effective affordance that encourages Victorian and Edwardian 'ghostly presences. Barthes (1993) has said that "the photograph does not necessarily say *what is no longer*, but only and for certain *what has been*" (1993:85).

Past photographs of guests serve as affording 'invitations' for 'ghostly presence'. It indicates "what has been" <u>still</u> remains at Bedford Springs because the affordance is still strong and influential in encouraging manifestations. Taking photographs today by today's guests will afford meaning for the 'ghosts' who are apparently aware of the camera's presence and function. This is because the camera and photographs are part of the ghost's experience and memory of Bedford Springs.

Photo 36: Personal Photography at Bedford Springs

Playing cards, and other table games, are another affordance. They resonate with past acts, and in some instances, were a 'liberating', and unique experience for Victorian women, who normally were 'silent' and confined to the domestic setting.

Photo 37: Table Games at Bedford Springs

There are many other activities, performed today, that serve as affordances for past 'ghostly presences' that remain attached to Bedford Springs. For more examples of these, please see (Sabol 2017b) for those specific affordances that may be meaningful for Late Victorian/Early Edwardian 'ghosts' at Bedford Springs.

A Final Note: 'Excavating' the Bedford Springs Hauntings

Period-defining objects and tour presentations as affordances exist as 'period pieces'. They still invite contemporary guests to experience the presence of the past at Bedford Springs. However, these historical affordances can attract or repel; certain behaviors if (and only if) the 'ghosts' perceive them.

Manifestations of 'ghostly presence' at Bedford Springs, with an emphasis on its Victorian Period (1830-1900) does appear to 'invite' ghosts, as indicated by the number of Victorian-era ghosts that are perceived to haunt there (see Sabol 2017b). The ghost tour, since inception, have increased haunting phenomena at Bedford Springs. This occurs both during the tour, and the experiences of tour participants afterwards.

A haunting, however, does not operate in uniform ways across contexts. There is no law-like construct, no secret code to unravel or 'debunk' a haunting. A haunting takes shape, and has meaning, through the interrelationship of context-specific artifacts, technology, performance, and the perception of the socio-cultural environment. This interrelationship 'invites', not predicts, 'ghostly presences' to materialize. Thus, affordances, operating at the intersection of artifacts, actors, and situations (scenarios) (Chemero 2003), can provide meaning that stimulates a haunting.

An investigation into the hauntings at Bedford Springs must use similar affordance relationalities, ones that encourage a particular strata or layer of memory to emerge, such as the Victorian Period at Bedford Springs. At the same time, the investigation must avoid affordances that 'discourage' context-specific materializations, such as the use of most contemporary 'ghost hunting' equipment. Such a technology was unknown in the Victorian period, and thus not part of past experience and memory.

Culture is an important factor here. Certain objects present themselves as serving a single function (or affordance). The many Victorian-era photographs, displayed throughout the Bedford Springs complex, function as an affordance to appear in contemporary photos, like in the past. Is that why both staff and guests have photographed 'ghosts', especially in certain places, such as the indoor pool?

Photography affords a relationality between a 'unique' space (and experience) (the indoor pool as the first, or one of the first, in the country) and photography. Such relationalities help us to determine, and further 'excavate', whether and when a particular affordance, such as the use of photography as a 'social affordance' (or the indoor pool as a 'affordance space') 'invites' a ghostly presence.

Much more research is needed, however, in order to understand the nature of the Bedford Springs 'haunting' experience. We must be careful how this research and investigation proceeds. We must not use affordances that discourage a 'ghost' to manifest, or one that disrupts past social codes and etiquette.

This concept of culture extends the notion of affordances to include a particular culture's sensory modalities in particular situations, such as rituals and 'rites of passage' (such as 'marriage proposals'). This links the physical environment to sensory agencies. Thus, this affects the way sensual processing is shaped by the 'ghost's' traditional repertoire of sensory abilities, in accordance with a phenomenology of sensation (actions that make sense to them, the visual sense of taking photographs, for example).

Our research into the hauntings at Bedford Springs, especially those of the Victorian and Early Edwardian Period, continues. If you have an experience during you stay at Bedford Springs, please let us know. We would welcome your input, and possibly include your encounter (with your permission) in our research.

You can contact us at: cuicospirit@hotmail.com; or

meg_garofalo2002@yahoo.com.

Bibliography

Barthes, Roland. 1993. *Camera Lucida: Reflections on Photography.* Translated by Richard Howard. New York: Hill and Wang.

Braude, Stephen E. 1991. Apparitions in *The Limits of Influence: Psychokinesis and the Philosophy of Science.* Edited by Stephen E. Braude. London: Routledge. pp. 170-218.

Chemero, A. 2003. An Outline of a Theory of Affordances. *Ecological Psychology* 15 (2): 181-195.

Costall Alan and Ann Richards. 2013. Canonical Affordances: The Psychology of Everyday Things in *The Oxford Handbook of the Archaeology of the Contemporary World.* Edited by Paul Graves-Brown, Rodney Harrison, and Angela Piccini. Oxford: Oxford University Press. pp. 82-93.

DeCerteau, M. 1984. *The Practice of Everyday Life.* Berkeley: University of California Press.

Dickerson, Vanessa D. 1996. *Victorian Ghosts in the Noontide: Women Writers and the Supernatural.* Columbia, Missouri: University of Missouri Press.

Gosden, Chris and Yvonne Marshall. 1999. The Cultural Biography of Objects. *World Archaeology* Vol. 31, No. 2 pp. 169-178.

Reynolds, James. 1955. *Ghosts in American Houses.* New York: Farrar, Straus, and Cudany.

Sabol, John G. 2016. *The Haunting of the Omni Bedford Springs Resort and Spa.* Bedford, Pennsylvania: Ghost Excavator Books, Inc.

2017a. *The Haunting Presences of the Omni Bedford Springs.* Bedford, Pennsylvania: Ghost Excavator Books, Inc.

2017b. *Victorian Ghosts of the Omni Bedford Springs: Representation and Reveal.* Bedford: Pennsylvania: Ghost Excavator Books, Inc.

About the Author

John Sabol is an archaeologist, cultural anthropologist, actor, and author. As an archaeologist, he has unearthed past material remains in excavations and site surveys in England, Mexico, and at various sites in the United States (including Eastern South Dakota, the Tennessee River Valleys, and in Pennsylvania). His anthropological fieldwork includes the studies of "spirits" in the religious beliefs of the afterlife among various cultural groups in Mexico (Mixtec, Zapotec, Lacandon, Nahuatl, and Otomi). His acting career includes "ghosting" performances of various characters and scenarios in more than 35 movies, TV shows, and documentaries. He has appeared in the A&E TV series, Paranormal State as an investigative consultant. He has written over thirty books.

His recent speaking engagements include the T.A.G. (Theoretical Archaeology Group) Conference at the University of California, Berkeley, at the Space and Place Conference in Prague, Czech Republic, the TAG Conference at the University in Buffalo, New York, Exploring the Extraordinary Conference in York, England, the C.H.A.T. archaeological conference also in York, and the GHost Conference at the University of London, London, England.

His investigative reports have been published in such diverse venues as Haunted Times Magazine, Tennessee Anthropologist, and the online journal, ParaAnthropology. He has been a frequent guest on numerous radio and internet talk shows, among them, Beyond the Edge Radio, The Paranormal View, Para X Radio, Blog Talk Radio, The Grand Dark Conspiracy, and Rusty O'Nhiall's "Mysterious and Unexplained" on PsiFM (Australia). He was a university professor in Mexico for 11 years, teaching both undergraduate and graduate courses on the anthropology of tourism. He has also been featured on public educational TV for U.S. and foreign markets, and has worked on international educational documentaries (in Spain).

He has a M.A. in Anthropology/Archaeology (University of Tennessee), and a B.A. in Sociology/Anthropology (Bloomsburg University). He has also attended Penn State University, the University of Pittsburgh, the University of the Americas (Cholula, Puebla, Mexico), and has studied theatre and method acting in Mexico City.

He can be reached via email at cuicospirit@hotmail.com. His website is: **www.ghostexcavation.com** and he can be found on Facebook ("Ghost Excavations with John Sabol").